A FRIEND IN THE LIBRARY

JUVENILE LITERATURE

BY

EVA MARCH TAPPAN

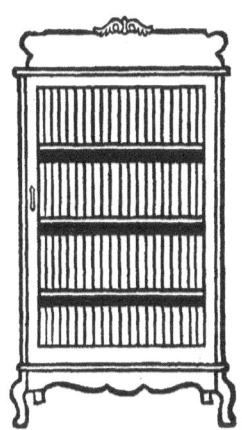

British Library Cataloguing-in-Publication Data
A catalogue record for this book is available from the
British Library

JUVENILE LITERATURE

A FRIEND IN THE LIBRARY

A Practical Guide to the Writings of

RALPH WALDO EMERSON

NATHANIEL HAWTHORNE

HENRY WADSWORTH LONGFELLOW

JAMES RUSSELL LOWELL

JOHN GREENLEAF WHITTIER

OLIVER WENDELL HOLMES

IN TWELVE VOLUMES

VOLUME VII

Eva March Tappan

Eva March Tappan was born on 26th December 1854 in Blackstone, Massachusetts, America. She is well known as a factual as well as fictional writer, but spent her early career as a teacher. Tappan was the only child of Reverend Edmund March Tappan and Lucretia Logée, and received her education at the esteemed Vassar College. This was a private coeducational liberal arts college, in the town of Poughkeepsie, New York, from which she graduated in 1875. Here, Tappan was a member of Phi Beta Kappa, the oldest honour society for the liberal arts and sciences, widely considered as the nations most prestigious society. She also edited the *Vassar Miscellany,* a college publication.

After leaving her early education, Tappan began teaching at Wheaton College, one of the oldest institutions of higher education for women in the United States, founded in 1834 and based in Norton, Massachusetts. She taught Latin and German here, from 1875 until 1880, before moving on to the Raymond Academy in Camden, New Jersey where she was associate Principal until 1894. Tappan also received a graduate degree in English Literature from the University of Pennsylvania. This allowed her to pursue her first love, that of reading and writing, and she taught as head of the English department at the English High School at Worcester, Massachusetts.

It was only after this date that Tappan began her literary career, writing about famous characters in history, often aimed at educating children in important historical themes and epochs. Some of her better known works include, *In the Days of William the Conqueror* (1901) and *In the Days of Queen Elizabeth* (1902), *The Out-of-Door Book* (1907), *When Knights Were Bold* (1911) and *The Little Book of the Flag* (1917). Tappan never married, being a happy singleton, and died on 29th January 1930, aged seventy-five.

JUVENILE LITERATURE

ONE day the famous romancer, Nathaniel Hawthorne, decided to write a book for children. He had two children of his own, and as he wrote story after story, he read each to them. They liked the tales so well that, before the manuscript was sent to the printer, they knew most of them by heart. After the book had been published, other children, too, were so pleased with it that they clamored for another, and Hawthorne wrote one for them. He liked the two volumes as much as they, and he said that he never did anything else so well.

These two books were "A Wonder-Book" and "Tanglewood Tales" (xiii.). They tell the stories that the Greeks who lived at least twenty-seven hundred years ago, and no one knows how much longer, really believed. There is the story of the golden apples that grew in the Garden of the Hesperides; of old Philemon and Baucis, who made two weary travelers as comfortable as their poverty would permit, and never guessed how Jupiter and Mercury — the unknown wanderers — would reward them. Another story is of Cadmus and his sowing dragon's teeth which came up as armed men. Each one of these myths is interesting; and, moreover, everybody ought to know them because they are so often referred to in literature and conversation. When Longfellow, for instance, is writing about Portland, Maine, where he lived as a boy, "the beautiful town that is seated by the sea," he speaks of

Islands that were the Hesperides
Of all my boyish dreams.

If you have read Hawthorne's "The Three Golden Apples" (xiii. 121) you know that the Garden of the Hesperides was the place where some golden apples were kept, and that they were guarded by a dragon with one hundred heads. Then you understand that when Longfellow was a boy, he thought of the charming islands of Casco Bay as a sort of enchanted country where one might find wonderful treasures and meet with marvelous adventures. If you do not know about the Hesperides, you lose all this. Again, one person sometimes says of another, "He has been sowing the dragon's teeth." Then if you know the story of Cadmus, you will understand the meaning of the speech, namely, that the person has been doing something which will get him into unexpected trouble.

Another book that Hawthorne wrote expressly for boys and girls is "Grandfather's Chair" (vol. xii.). This is a collection of stories of early American history. There are many such collections, but Hawthorne knew how to choose stories that are interesting and how to tell them so charmingly that they seem fresh and new. One is about John Hull, who made the pine-tree shillings for the colonists, and gave his daughter's weight in silver shillings for her dowry (xii. 37). Another is about Sir William Phipps, who longed to build a "fair brick house" on Green Lane in Boston, and of the vast treasure that he discovered in a sunken vessel at the bottom of the ocean (xii. 68).

A third volume is of biographies (vol. xii.). Here among others is the story of the little Quaker boy who had never heard of such an art as picture-making, but who drew so good a likeness of his baby-sister that his mother recognized it at a glance. He was only "little Ben" in those days, but he became the famous artist, Benjamin West.

Hawthorne wrote many other stories that had nothing to do with either history or biography; but every one has a meaning. That is why people read them over and over and think about them. "Little Daffydowndilly" (iii. 281), for instance, is a simple story of a very little boy, but it has a big meaning. "The Great Stone Face" (iii. 29) is the story of a face of rock on a mountain-side and of a prophecy that some time a child should be born who would resemble it and who would become "the greatest and noblest personage of his time." This has a meaning which is even greater than that of "Daffydowndilly." "The Snow-Image" (iii. 1) is a charming story of two children and the pretty little maiden that they made of snow. It is simple enough for even very small children to enjoy, but its meaning is deep enough for exceedingly wise grown folk to ponder over.

Longfellow wrote at least two poems expressly for children. One is "The Three Kings" (iii. 122), the "Wise men" who came out of the East, —

> And they travelled by night and they slept by day,
> For their guide was a beautiful, wonderful star.

Onward they rode until they came to Bethlehem, —

And cradled there in the scented hay,
  In the air made sweet by the breath of kine,
The little child in the manger lay,
The child, that would be king one day
  Of a kingdom not human but divine.

So it was that the Three Kings found the Christ-Child.

The second poem has quite a long story. When the poet was a young professor in Harvard College, he wrote "The Village Blacksmith" (ii. 72), a poem about a smithy "Under a spreading chestnut tree" not far from his home. The chestnut tree was finally cut down. Longfellow was exceedingly sorry, and some of his friends planned a way to make him feel that the old tree was not wholly lost. They asked the children of the public schools of Cambridge if they would like to give him

7

a chair made of the wood of the tree. They were delighted at the suggestion. The chair was made, and forty years after he wrote "The Village Blacksmith," part of the chestnut tree came to him, "shaped as a stately chair." Longfellow was greatly pleased. He wrote the poem, "From My Arm-Chair" (iii. 220), and gave a copy to every child who came to see the chair. He wrote: —

> And thus, dear children, have ye made for me
>   This day a jubilee,
> And to my more than threescore years and ten
>   Brought back my youth again.

The Cambridge children were happy indeed to find that they had given "their poet" so much pleasure.

Longfellow wrote many poems about children. One of them is especially beautiful, and is especially interesting because it is about himself as a boy. It is "My Lost Youth" (iii. 39), the poem that mentions the "islands that were the Hesperides." He writes of the very things that a boy would be most likely to remember, — the "sea-tides tossing free," the fort on the hill with its bugle call and its sunrise gun, the sea-fight that "thundered o'er the bay," and "the shadows of Deering's Woods." Deering's Woods has now become a public park, and over the fireplace in a little rest-house beside the pond the closing stanza of the poem is written : —

And Deering's Woods are fresh and fair,
  And with joy that is almost pain
My heart goes back to wander there,
And among the dreams of the days that were,
  I find my lost youth again.
    And the strange and beautiful song,

A FRIEND IN THE LIBRARY

The groves are repeating it still:
"A boy's will is the wind's will,
And the thoughts of youth are long, long thoughts."

Longfellow had children of his own, and it was about them that he wrote "The Children's Hour" (iii. 63) : —

> Between the dark and the daylight,
>> When the night is beginning to lower,
> Comes a pause in the day's occupations,
>> That is known as the Children's Hour.

He tells us of his three little girls coming softly down the stairs to take him by surprise. We can almost see them as

> By three doors left unguarded
>> They enter my castle wall!

> They climb up into my turret
>> O'er the arms and back of my chair;
> If I try to escape, they surround me;
>> They seem to be everywhere.

"The Wreck of the Hesperus" (i. 69) is about the shipwreck of a little girl whose eyes were blue

> as the fairy flax,
> Her cheeks like the dawn of day;

and even in "Hiawatha" (ii. 123), the story of an Indian brave, the poet writes a charming account of Hiawatha's boyhood and tells us that

> Of all beasts he learned the language,
> Learned their names and all their secrets,
> How the beavers built their lodges,
> Where the squirrels hid their acorns,
> How the reindeer ran so swiftly,
> Why the rabbit was so timid,
> Talked with them where'er he met them,
> Called them "Hiawatha's Brothers."

One hardly knows when to stop talking about Longfellow's poems, for there are so many of them that young folk like. In the "Tales of a Wayside Inn" (iv. 13–285) is a whole group of story-telling poems. Here is the famous "Paul Revere's Ride," and you can almost hear the beat of the horse's hoofs as the hero gallops out into the darkness to warn the Massachusetts farmers of the coming of the British. Another of the Tales is about the meeting of the man whose

> Favorite pastime was to slay the deer
> In summer on some Adirondac hill, —

with the other great folk of the village of Killingworth, and their decree that all the birds should be killed. The poem goes on to tell what happened, and what the repentant farmers did to try to make up for their blunder. Then, too, among these Tales is the poem for Sunday afternoon, "The Legend

Beautiful" (iv. 185); and there is "The Bell of Atri," the story of the much abused horse who took the prevention of cruelty to animals into his own charge.

> He calls for justice, being sore distressed,
> And pleads his cause as loudly as the best.

Longfellow has written many poems that children love for their sound, like "The Old Clock on the Stairs" (i. 257) and "The Building of the Ship" (i. 277). A child will find in each of these enough of a story to be clear and interesting; and by and by, when he is older, he will see how true they are. That is one of the great beauties of Longfellow's poems, namely, that they seem to grow as the reader grows. A child may read them and learn them by heart and think he knows all that they mean, but if he reads them again when he is older, he will find that there is more in them than he had discovered, that some verse that he had looked upon as only painting a pretty picture is really full of thought which he is glad to have brought to his mind.

If you open volume twelve of the works of Holmes, you will see in the frontispiece the portrait of a gentleman who looks as if he had just thought of something amusing, and was all ready to tell you about it. He is in no hurry, however, and he has a fashion of beginning a poem as if he were in a most serious mood, and you must expect a seven-headed sermon at least. Then, before you know it, he has flashed in some merry thought. In "Contentment" (xii. 414), for instance, he begins gravely, —

Little I ask; my wants are few;
　　I only wish a hut of stone, —

and then he adds, —

　　(A *very plain* brown stone will do)
　　　That I may call my own; —
　　And close at hand is such a one,
　　In yonder street that fronts the sun.

And so he goes on through the poem, beginning each stanza with the utmost seriousness
and then expressing his immoderate wishes in
most moderate fashion. He says: —

　　Jewels are baubles; 't is a sin
　　　To care for such unfruitful things; —
　　One good-sized diamond in a pin, —
　　　Some, *not so large*, in rings, —
　　A ruby, and a pearl, or so,
　　Will do for me; — I laugh at show.

And he closes, declaring that he is

A FRIEND IN THE LIBRARY

Grateful for the blessing lent
Of simple tastes and mind content!

If five thousand people were asked which
poem of Holmes came to their minds first at
the mention of his name, I fancy that at least
four thousand of them would answer, "'The
One-Hoss Shay.'" "The Deacon's Master-
piece," Holmes calls it (xii. 417). He describes the deacon's sober reasoning that —

In building of chaises, I tell you what,
There is always *somewhere* a weakest spot, —
In hub, tire, felloe, in spring or thill,
In panel, or crossbar, or floor, or sill,
In screw, bolt, thoroughbrace, — lurking still,
Find it somewhere you must and will, —
Above or below, or within or without, —
And that's the reason, beyond a doubt,
That a chaise *breaks down*, but does n't *wear out.*

The deacon determines to make one chaise
that shall never break down.

> "Fur," said the Deacon, " 't 's mighty plain
> Thut the weakes' place mus' stan' the strain;
> 'N' the way t' fix it, uz I maintain,
>   Is only jest
> T' make that place uz strong uz the rest."

So the deacon built his "shay," which
"ran a hundred years to a day," and then —
but Holmes tells the story better than any-
body else could, and one must not infringe
upon his privileges.

So it is that Holmes writes when he gives us
pure fun; but he can do more than this, for he
can write a poem that makes us smile one
moment and wink fast the next moment.
Some of these poems were written for the re-
unions of the Class of 1829 of Harvard Col-

lege — fortunate class that it was to have such a member! The most famous of them is "The Boys" (xii. 303). It was written thirty years after his graduation day. "The Boys" are the classmates, and he says: —

We've a trick, we young fellows, you may have been
    told,
Of talking (in public) as if we were old: —
That boy we call "Doctor," and this we call "Judge";
It's a neat little fiction, — of course it's all fudge.

The author of "America" was a classmate, and Holmes says of him: —

And there's a nice youngster of excellent pith, —
Fate tried to conceal him by naming him Smith;
But he shouted a song for the brave and the free, —
Just read on his medal, "My country, — of thee."

The poem closes: —

Then here's to our boyhood, its gold and its gray!
The stars of its winter, the dews of its May!

And when we have done with our life-lasting toys,
Dear Father, take care of thy children, THE BOYS!

The greatest of Holmes's poems, "The Chambered Nautilus" (xii. 393), was written for grown folk, I suppose, but it always seemed to me that it belonged rather to the younger folk, because it is a poem of growth, and they are the ones that are growing most rapidly. The nautilus lives at first in a little shell, but adds each year a larger cell to the spiral, moves into that, and knows "the old no more." Holmes tells us this in beautiful verse, and closes: —

Build thee more stately mansions, O my soul,
  As the swift seasons roll!
  Leave thy low-vaulted past!
Let each new temple, nobler than the last,
Shut thee from heaven with a dome more vast,

Till thou at length art free,
Leaving thine outgrown shell by life's unresting sea!

When Holmes was seventy-nine years old, he made a summer trip to Europe. While he was in London, the Princess of Wales, now Queen Alexandra, sent him her autograph album with the request that he would write his name and a stanza from one of his poems. This stanza from "The Chambered Nautilus" is the one that he chose, and he copied it into the royal album, "as I have often done for plain republican albums," he said.

When Holmes wrote prose, he wrote it for grown folk, but at least one piece of it has been seized upon by the young people. That is "My Hunt after the Captain" (viii. 16). "The Captain" was his son, who had been wounded in battle, and Holmes tells the story of the search, from the coming of the telegram to the happy meeting on board the train. There is another bit of prose that maybe boys and girls do not read; but I am sure that they would if it were not sandwiched in between two medical essays. It is called "Cinders from the Ashes" (viii. 239); but it has nothing to do with either cinders or ashes, for it gives the writer's memories of the time when he and the other boys of Cambridge went to school at Cambridgeport with the "Port-chucks," as the "Cambridge-chucks" called them.

Lowell has some poems that children like and claim as their own. One is the touching "First Snow-Fall" (xii. 167), wherein the little Mabel asks, "Father, who makes it snow?" The father is thinking of a tiny mound in the cemetery, —

How the flakes are folding it gently,
As did robins the babes in the wood.

He tells the child about the coming of the snow : —

Then, with eyes that saw not, I kissed her;
And she, kissing back, could not know
That my kiss was given to her sister,
Folded close under deepening snow.

Another of his poems is called "For an Autograph" (xii. 177), and I fancy that two of its stanzas have been written in more albums than any other lines. They are not especially original, but they express extremely well what some other people have thought. These two stanzas are : —

Life is a leaf of paper white
Whereon each one of us may write
His word or two, and then comes night.

. . . .

Greatly begin! though thou have time
But for a line, be that sublime, —
Not failure, but low aim is crime.

There is one poem of Lowell's that every
boy ought to know by heart, one that every
girl should learn, and one that both ought to
read over and over again till they love every
line of it. The poem for the boys is called
"The Heritage" (ix. 47). It begins: —

The rich man's son inherits lands,
    And piles up brick and stone, and gold,
And he inherits soft white hands,
    And tender flesh that fears the cold,
    Nor dares to wear a garment old;
A heritage, it seems to me,
One scarce would wish to hold in fee.

This sounds as if the poor man's son had the
better of it, and so Lowell believes; but before

23

the poem has closed, he shows what the rich
man's son may do to make himself of as much
value as the poor man's son, and ends, —

> A heritage, it seems to me,
> Worth being rich to hold in fee.

The poem for girls is called "My Love"
(ix. 18). It gives Lowell's idea of a true wo-
man; and his idea is so beautiful and so noble
that every line of his description is well worth
remembering. The finest stanza of all is, —

> She doeth little kindnesses,
> Which most leave undone, or despise:
> For naught that sets one heart at ease,
> And giveth happiness or peace,
> Is low-esteemèd in her eyes.

The poem for both boys and girls is "The
Vision of Sir Launfal" (ix. 301). It belongs
to them, first, because it is a story; second,

because it has a meaning that is worth much to grown folk, but worth far more to young people; third, because so large a part of it is written about things that young folk know, and one cannot help finding it interesting to compare what Lowell says with what he himself has seen and thought. Read his description of a June day, and notice whether you have seen the same things that he has, and whether you feel as he says one does feel on such a day. Read the Prelude to Part Second, and, if it is winter, break through the ice of some little half-frozen brook, and find out for yourselves whether Lowell was right in saying that on the under-side are "silvery mosses that downward grew." See whether there really are "diamond drops" on the tops of the bulrushes. Compare Part First and

Part Second. See whether the crows flop "by twos and threes" in the summer, while you see "A single crow on the tree-top bleak" in the winter, or whether Lowell said this to make nature sympathize with the story. And at the end of the poem, stop a little and think what it means translated into twentieth-century thinking; that is, what would a young man of to-day who was as brave and honest as Sir Launfal seek to do? What sort of life would he lead? What would he do for himself and for others? That is one way to make a poem your own.

So many of Whittier's poems are simple and homelike that boys and girls have always been fond of them. One poem, "Snow-Bound" (ii. 134), is especially beloved because it is full of pictures of home-life in the country. Whittier does not borrow any fine words for his poem; he writes about the "chores," the "corn-crib," the "brush-pile," "the huskings and the apple-bees."

Another poem, "The Barefoot Boy" (ii. 126), pictures the poet himself when he was a boy, and tells of his discoveries : —

> How the tortoise bears his shell,
> How the woodchuck digs his cell,
> And the ground-mole sinks his well;
> How the robin feeds her young,
> How the oriole's nest is hung.

Whittier could write such strong, stirring poems as "Ichabod" (iv. 61), which was his protest against the Fugitive Slave Law, written in one of the saddest moments of his life, he said; but he loved peace and quiet, and it is pleasanter to think of him as writing of his memories of the country life that he loved so well. Another of his poems about country boyhood is "In School-Days" (ii. 162), which describes the kind of schoolhouse in which he must have learned his first lessons, even if the story of the little girl who was sorry that she spelled the word, because she hated to go above him, was only a fancy. Often he writes of "grown-up" life in the country, as in "Among the Hills" (i. 260), but it is always the country that he knows, the mountains that he has loved and watched.

> Through Sandwich notch the west-wind sang
>   Good morrow to the cotter;
> And once again Chocorua's horn
>   Of shadow pierced the water.

All is simple and earnest and straightforward — and also beautiful. "Maud Muller"

(i. 148) is a country idyl. In this poem is the famous couplet, —

> For of all sad words of tongue or pen,
> The saddest are these: "It might have been!"

Whittier often wrote of some legend or incident that touched him, most frequently of some old tale of the country about his own home. For instance, a shipwrecked sailor who had wandered away into a desert and suffered terribly from thirst made a vow to God that if he ever reached home, he would dig a well by the roadside for wayfarers. Whittier made a poem of this, "The Captain's Well" (iv. 289). "The Wishing Bridge" (i. 398) is another of his home legends, wherein two school-girls "wished," one to see the world, and one to be a queen. The poem tells how it came about that each had her wish, though in quite different fashion from what she had hoped.

Whittier did not have the advantages of college life and travel that were enjoyed by the others of our six authors; but he read and studied and thought, and so won an education for himself. In his "Proem" (i. 11) he speaks of "The harshness of an untaught ear"; and yet in this very "Proem" is one of the most musical stanzas in the language: —

I love the old melodious lays
Which softly melt the ages through,
    The songs of Spenser's golden days,
    Arcadian Sidney's silvery phrase,
Sprinkling our noon of time with freshest morning
    dew.

Emerson was a philosopher as well as a poet. Some one once asked a famous Greek

named Pythagoras, "What is a philosopher?"
and he replied: "At the games some try to win
glory, some buy and sell for money, and some
watch what the others do. So it is in life; and
philosophers are those who watch, who study
nature, and search for wisdom." Emerson
did these three things, — he watched, he
studied nature, and he searched for wisdom.
Moreover, he put what he had seen and
thought, sometimes into verse and sometimes
into prose. He loved nature so sincerely that
he could hardly help writing about the trees
and flowers and brooks as if they were dear
friends. He saw like a naturalist, but he told
what he had seen like a poet. He saw that
many flowers have five petals, and he wrote,
"Nature loves the number five." He saw that
rivers flow into the sea, and he wrote: —

The river knows the way to the sea.

These lines are from "Woodnotes" (ix. 43), and it is full of such bits of poetic knowledge as these. He loved beautiful things, and in "The Rhodora" (ix. 37), is his famous line, —

Then Beauty is its own excuse for being.

He loves a storm as well as a flower, and his "The Snow-Storm" (ix. 41) is one of the best descriptions of a storm that have ever been written. The first line, —

Announced by all the trumpets of the sky, —

sounds like the mighty blasts of a coming tempest. A little further on in the poem is a phrase which no one else has used, but it expresses perfectly the feeling that all the world is shut out which comes to us in a heavy snow-fall: —

> The housemates sit
> Around the radiant fireplace, enclosed
> In *a tumultuous privacy of storm.*

Every one likes Emerson's "Fable" (ix. 75):

> The mountain and the squirrel
> Had a quarrel
> And the former called the latter "Little Prig."

There is a tiny poem, "Letters" (ix. 217), which ought to be put up over every mailbox: —

> Every day brings a ship,
> Every ship brings a word;
> Well for those that have no fear,
> Looking seaward well assured
> That the word the vessel brings
> Is the word they wish to hear.

"The Concord Hymn" (ix. 158) is familiar: —

By the rude bridge that arched the flood;

but the "Boston Hymn" (ix. 201), though not quite so well known, is wonderfully good. It is simple and sensible and full of the spirit of the early days of our country; and there are thoughts in it that one who reads it can never forget. The first stanza is a noble one: —

> The word of the Lord by night
> To the watching Pilgrims came,
> As they sat by the seaside,
> And filled their hearts with flame.

There is something about Emerson's poems that is different from those of any other writer. The way to love them is to learn them by heart. In the works of most poets we can find much to enjoy by merely a single reading; but in Emerson's there is some mysterious quality, I do not know what, that makes them seem finer and nobler when one can say them aloud or whisper them to one's self without the book.

Emerson's prose is chiefly essays and lectures. These names do not sound very tempting to young folk, and yet I have sometimes thought that much of Emerson's prose belongs to boys and girls, only they have not all discovered it. In his essay on "Country Life" (xii. 135), for instance, there are three or four paragraphs describing the walks that the botanist Linnæus used to take, and telling what wonderful discoveries he made simply by keeping his eyes open. Those surely belong to the sharp-eyed young people. The essay on Thoreau (x. 451) is so good that I believe boys and girls would like every page of it. Indeed, no one could help being interested

in Emerson's account of his friend, for Thoreau was a most interesting man. None of the
wild animals was afraid of him. Emerson
tells us that "fishes swam into his hand, and
he took them out of the water." Nature hid
nothing from him. One day, walking with a
stranger, who inquired where Indian arrow-
heads could be found, he replied, "Every-
where," and, stooping forward, picked one on
the instant from the ground.

Not only are Emerson's essays on people
and on country life well worth while for boys
and girls, but there are also many thoughts in
some of those whose titles may not seem to
them especially promising. In "Compensa-
tion," for instance (ii. 93), it is good to find
out what he means by "Every act rewards
itself," — "All things are double," "The

borrower runs in his own debt," — "The thief steals from himself." These are only snatches of the essay, but they are wise thoughts. It is a good thing to decide what you think they mean; then find them in the essay and see what Emerson has to say about them. There is so much in his writings, that one can give only hints and suggestions of its riches. The best way to become acquainted with them is to turn the pages of some essay, and whenever a sentence catches your eye, stop and read it. The chances are that before long you will feel as if you would like to begin at the beginning and read the whole paper; and when you have read it, you will find that you have grown, for you have gained some wise, strong thoughts that you have never had before.

ADDITIONAL

HAWTHORNE

The Gray Champion, i. 1.
Endicott and the Red Cross, ii. 276.
Feathertop, iv. 312.

LONGFELLOW

The Phantom Ship, iii. 18.
The Discoverer of the North Cape, iii. 52.
Christmas Bells, iii. 139.
The Two Rivers, iii. 234.
A Psalm of Life, i. 19.
Rain in Summer, i. 227.
The Day is Done, i. 246.
The Builders, i. 305.
Pegasus in Pound, i. 313.
The Skeleton in Armor, i. 63.
The Three Kings, iii. 122.
The Leap of Roushan Beg, iii. 117.

LOWELL

The Fountain, ix. 33.
To the Dandelion, ix. 230.

Dara, xii. 165.
The Singing Leaves, xii. 169.
The Changeling, ix. 251.

WHITTIER

The Poet and the Children, iv. 150.
Kallundborg Church, iv. 265.
The Exiles, i. 53.
The Pipes at Lucknow, i. 183.
Rhymed Letter to Lucy Larcom, iv. 405.
The Heroine of Long Point, v. 428.
David Matson, v. 314.
The King's Missive, i. 381.
The Poet and the Children, iv. 150.
The Wreck of Rivermouth, iv. 235.
My Playmate, i. 238.
King Solomon and the Ants, i. 369.
Nauhaught, the Deacon, i. 304.
The Robin, i. 314.
King Volmer and Elsie, i. 345.
The Brown Dwarf of Rügen, i. 421.
Red Riding Hood, ii. 166.

HOLMES

Old Ironsides, xii. 1.

The Dorchester Giant, xii. 19.
The September Gale, xii. 29.
Bill and Joe, xii. 287.
Dorothy Q., xiii. 47.
A Farewell to Agassiz, xiii. 96.
Grandmother's Story of the Bunker-Hill Battle, xiii. 149.
The Broomstick Train, xiii. 339.
The Spectre Pig, xiii. 392.
The Ballad of the Oysterman, xiii. 416.

EMERSON

The Humble-Bee, ix. 38.
Forbearance, ix. 83.
Boston, ix. 212.
Translation from Ali Ben Abu Taleb, ix. 302.
Wealth, vi. 85.
Behavior, vi. 169.
Stonehenge, v. 273.
Manners, iii. 119.
Farming, vii. 137.
Books, vii. 189.

JUVENILE LITERATURE

QUESTIONS

1. Which of the six authors wrote most works expressly for children?
   Hawthorne.

2. Why is it worth while to read the stories of the old Greek myths?
   Because they are beautiful and because they so often explain literature and conversation.

3. Why do grown people enjoy Hawthorne's stories for children?
   Because they are so full of meaning.

4. Why are so many of Longfellow's poems adapted to children's reading?
   Because they are simple and clear and written on familiar subjects.

5. Which poem of Longfellow's is written about his own boyhood?
   "My Lost Youth" (iii. 39).

6. Why is "The Building of the Ship" (i. 77) of special interest?

   Because it is a beautiful "labor poem," and because it has a double significance, the ship and the "Ship of State."

7. What is the "framework" of "The Tales of a Wayside Inn" (iv. 11)?

   A group of friends meet at an old inn and tell stories.

8. What three kinds of poems has Holmes written?

   Those that amuse; those that amuse and touch; and those that show thought and reflection.

9. Which is Holmes's most amusing poem?

   "The One-Hoss Shay" (xii. 417).

10. Which is his best poem of thought?

    "The Chambered Nautilus" (xii. 393).

11. Which poem gave Holmes his earliest fame?

    "Old Ironsides" (xii. 2).

12. Which poem of Lowell's is especially good for boys?

    "The Heritage" (ix. 47).

13. Which presents a noble ideal for girls?

    "My Love" (i. 18).

14. Why is "The Vision of Sir Launfal" (ix. 299) so general a favorite?

    Because of its beauty and accurate descriptions of nature, and because it is so full of meaning.

15. Why is Whittier's "Snow-Bound" (ii. 134) of historical value?

    Because it presents so perfect a picture of country life in the early part of the nineteenth century.

16. In which poem does Whittier picture his own boyhood?

    "The Barefoot Boy" (ii. 126).

43

17. What were some of Whittier's favorite sub-
    jects?

    Home-life, legends, nature, and religion.

18. Why is Emerson called a philosopher?

    *Because he watched life, he studied nature,
    and he searched for wisdom.*

19. Where may two excellent descriptions of
    snow-storms be found?

    *In Whittier's "Snow-Bound" (ii. 134)
    and in Emerson's "The Snow-Storm"
    (ix. 41).*

20. Why is it of special value to read Emerson's
    essays?

    *Because they are full of wise, strong
    thoughts that make one grow.*